Syberia THE WORLD BEFORE

Syberia The World Before ©2022 Microids SA. Author and Artistic Director: Benoit Sokal.
Music composed and arranged by Inon Zur. All rights reserved.

ISBN 978-1-70515-766-4

HAL•LEONARD®

7777 W. BLUEMOUND RD. P.O. BOX 13819 MILWAUKEE, WI 53213

Visit Hal Leonard Online at
www.halleonard.com

Contact us:
Hal Leonard
7777 West Bluemound Road
Milwaukee, WI 53213
Email: info@halleonard.com

In Europe, contact:
Hal Leonard Europe Limited
42 Wigmore Street
Marylebone, London, W1U 2RN
Email: info@halleonardeurope.com

In Australia, contact:
Hal Leonard Australia Pty. Ltd.
4 Lentara Court
Cheltenham, Victoria, 3192 Australia
Email: info@halleonard.com.au

CONTENTS

HYMN OF VAGHEN

By INON ZUR

THOSE LOST DAYS

By INON ZUR

KATE WALKER

By INON ZUR

Con moto

mp

mf

DREAMS TO BE BROKEN

By INON ZUR

A NICE PERSON

By INON ZUR

RISING FOR ADVENTURE

By INON ZUR

Heroically

DANA ROZE

By INON ZUR

FOUR LEGS

By INON ZUR

A QUIET PLACE

By INON ZUR

LEON KOBATIS

By INON ZUR

BITTER LIBERATION

By INON ZUR

SHATTERED DESTINY

By INON ZUR

With motion